Stories from My Youth

F.A. PFLUGHOEFT

authorHOUSE®

AuthorHouse™
1663 Liberty Drive
Bloomington, IN 47403
www.authorhouse.com
Phone: 1 (800) 839-8640

Published by AuthorHouse   11/20/2015

ISBN: 978-1-5049-6294-0 (sc)
ISBN: 978-1-5049-6295-7 (hc)
ISBN: 978-1-5049-6293-3 (e)

Print information available on the last page.

This book is printed on acid-free paper.

About the Author

F.A. Pflughoeft (Fritz) was born on August 15th, 1922 to Werner and Aurelia (Seehafer) Pflughoeft in Medford, WI. He had an adventurous childhood and high school career in Medford (as evidenced by his stories).

In fall 1940 he attended Marquette University and completed his degree in dentistry in 1945 (a special wartime dental course compressed i.e. no vacations except one day for Christmas, to provide dentists for the military). He served his country as a Lieutenant in the US Navy from graduation to 1947, spending most of that time in the Philippines.

Fritz married Roylee Ross on May 22, 1948 in Virginia, IL. After a couple years in private practice, Fritz joined the Veterans Administration Hospital system. This meant living in South Dakota, Wisconsin and Connecticut before returning to Wood VA Hospital in Milwaukee, WI in 1959. He continued his studies to become a board certified Prosthodontist and taught at Marquette Dental School part-time. He retired from the VA in 1977 and continued at Marquette for quite a few more years.

Fritz and Roylee have 3 children, Jane, Martha and John; 4 grandchildren, Rachel (Mildbrand) Klinner, Peter Klinner, Lauren and Dana Pflughoeft. At present they have one great-granddaughter, Carly Ross Mildbrand.

Fritz loved history and enjoyed taking pictures during his numerous travels to almost every part of the globe. At the time of publication, Fritz and Roylee are 93 and 92 years young and reside in Wauwatosa, WI.

A Day at the Lake 1933-1938

By Frederick August Pflughoeft

Sundays during the summer months frequently were celebrated, the weather permitting, with an outdoor picnic held usually on the lawn in front of the Musselman family cottage. The preparations were great – huge. Pies and cakes had been baked, a ham or chicken prepared. Sundays seemed to always be bright and warm. Some people drove out from town, others were living at the lake for the summer. Everyone came prepared with food.

When we were not 'staying out', the day started by loading Father's pick-up truck with food and materials for a project. There always were jobs to be completed at the cottage, repairs, making firewood for the fireplace, roadway to be patched, never an end to work.

Edith and I rode in the truck back sharing space with the other cargo. After arriving at the cottage and unloading and stowing the food and other general cargo, a trip to get ice was necessary. At that time our driveway was up the hill off Perkinstown Ave. The parking lot was on top of the hill behind the cottage. The most convenient way to get the ice for our 'icebox' was by boat. The ice house was located just behind the High View tavern and dance hall. The convenience of this route for obtaining the supply of ice was due to an impasse regarding driving over the lot to the east. The owner of this lot, a Mr. Spreen and Father were at loggerheads apparently for no known reason.

(The cottages were originally built without electricity. Bottled gas was the fuel used for cooking and lighting. Gas was piped to lamps hanging from the roof/rafters in the center of the cottages. It provided a very bright light (like Coleman white gas lanterns with mantles) for the whole cottage since the walls to the bedrooms didn't go up to the roof. Electricity replaced the gas for lighting whenever 'REA' (one of FDR's policies – Rural Electrification???) came in, possibly 1935ish? And within the cottages the electric wires probably followed the route of the gas pipes to the new light fixtures. JP)

So we went for ice by boat. Every cottage at that time had ice tongs. The saw dust used to preserve the ice was washed off and the rather slow task of rowing the ice to the cottage was complete.

Musselmans picked up their ice by car. Dick was in the process of learning to drive the car.

Now the preparations for the feast began in earnest.

Mr Musselman (Roy) with his megaphone walked out on Ungrodt's pier (now Ketelhut's) and called to Mrs. Fleming. The time for the picnic was set and any last minute instructions were settled upon.

Mr Musselman usually baked the ham or chicken at his bakery shop. Potato salads, fruit salads, pies and cakes were all prepared before hand.

Father and Mr Musselman had obtained two FISK tire advertising signs (Porcelain baked on heavy metal sheets approximately three by six feet) which made great table surfaces and easy to store and easy to clean. They also constructed wood horses to hold the signs. *(I remember these, do you? JP)*

By mealtime the improvised table was overflowing with good wholesome food, china plates and cups for coffee and glasses for iced tea and lemonade.

The party was made up of the cottages at the south-east corner of Lake Esadore, often referred to as the Deutsche Ecke (German Corner). Often times family friends from Medford were Sunday guests.

Cottages from the east to west along south east shore of Lake Esadore

Cottage family in 1930s	Cottage family in my memory (JP)
Lot owned by Mr Spreen, no cottage	Pflughoeft & Boyle
Pflughoeft	Jimmy/Jane& Tom/Holroyd/ Clark& Waldhart
Musselman	Musselman & Loucks

Ungrodt	Scharrschmidt/Ketelhut/ Ketelhut
Leicht	Scharrschmidt/Weister
Michler	Klingbeil/Klinner
Jacobson	??Lemke
Fleming	??

About this time Dick Musselman was asked to drive down to the Scaharrschmidt's family gas station and ice cream stand at the corner of highways E and 64,to pick up a gallon container of homemade ice cream. I, of course, had to accompany Dick to hold the ice cream container protectively on my lap.

Soon the time came to tidy up the eating area. Water (from the lake) was necessary to be heated for dish washing and other clean up chores. Dick had shown me how to climb up on the roof of the Musselman cottage to escape from cleaning up jobs, carry water, gather dishes, etc. We were unavailable thanks to this subterfuge.

Usually during the summer, we *(Fritz, Edith and their mother)* spent some time living at the lake. Since we had no telephone at the lake, Father would return home in the evening. He had to be available for service calls (as the local undertaker/Funeral Director).

Cottage life was fairly predictable. The Roe family, cousins to Rachel and Dick, usually spent several weeks as Musselman's guests. Swimming, canoe sailing and boating made for lots of summer fun.

Mrs. Musselman (Ora) was a very nice mother and friend to the Muzzy kids. Mr Musselman was a sort of pixyish personality. He had a cottage work day costume (swim suit) that consisted of a burlap potato sack with the bottom corners cut open for his legs and several circumferences of sash cord acted as a belt, allowing him to walk in and out of the water.

Father and Mr Musselman spent quite a bit of time and effort maintaining the shore line. As mentioned previously, our group of cottages were located at the southeastern corner of Lake Esadore, consequently the shore line required attention to repair erosion caused by wave action. *(from the prevailing winds out of the west?)*

Again I must mention that summers at the lake were great times. Our acquaintance grew into friendships which we all enjoyed for many years. To my way of thinking, the next generations seem to be carrying on as friends and all seem to enjoy time and happenings at the lake and otherwise.

Recollections by
Frederick A. Pflughoeft
2010

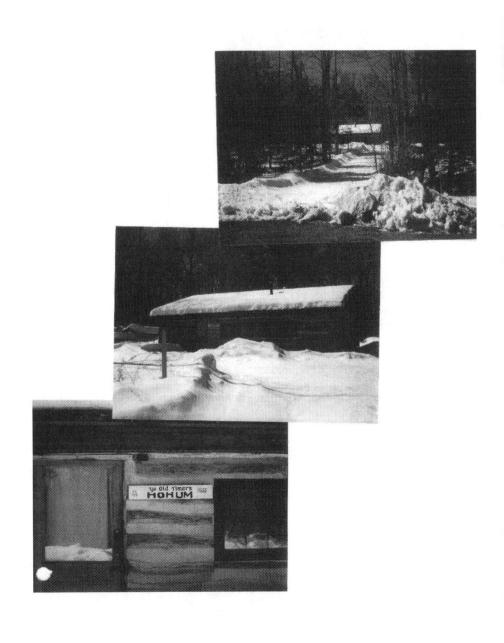

History of Ho Hum

By Fred Pflughoeft written 2001

Ho Hum is a deer camp-hunting cabin- lodge- hunting shanty- shanty in the Mondeaux section of the Chequamegan National Forest located in North Central Wisconsin.

My Father and his crew, which consisted of a group of friends living in Medford, hunted out of the Ho Hum for many years. The surrounding forest was mostly highlands which supported a hearty second growth of hardwood timber. Deer were quite numerous. The hunting area was pretty much described by the Yellow River on the west and the Mondeaux River on the east.

Originally their stumping grounds were inaccessible by road. F. R. (fire road) number 107 extended north from county highway M to a large sawmill. From here it was necessary to "pack in" to the hunting area. Very Soon F. R.

107 was extended north, abutting the 80 acre lot the group had learned to admire and subsequently acquired. The presence of a road made it possible to construct a building. This meant they could actually move into the forest and live there for the duration of the hunting season.

The rugged log cabin consisted of a large room with areas which satisfied sleeping, eating and resting in front of the large fireplace after a long days hunt.

When it came to building, it was decided that three of the gang would finance the enterprise but the entire group would forever be very welcome. The three men were: Roy Musselman, Charley Fleming and Father. This was a very prudent move and most fortuitous for us fellows.

The cabin site selected was on a little rise near a small stream in the midst of some large white pines. The floor plan was arranged for a sleeping area to accommodate twelve, the kitchen had a wood-burning cook stove with adequate cooking space. The large fireplace which centered the social area could accept a five-foot log.

Over the years the group included Gaylord Blakeslee, brothers Frank and Peanie Pierce, Gil Ungrodt, Lin Suits, Bill Schmidt, Vince Hirsch, Mose Piorer, Gil Strebig as well as the three mentioned above. Since Father and Mr. Muzzy were part of the original three, it allowed Dick and me access to the Ho Hum over the years. The access was granted as long as we were considerate of the place, kept the building clean and supplied with adequate firewood for the next users.

Dick always had good ideas and schemes. I remember working in the back of Father's furniture store on a Saturday morning when Dick came in and suggested some fellows really ought to spend the weekend at the Ho Hum. Getting permission from our dads was no problem. Over the years we had many good times camping at the Ho Hum with our group: Don Urquhardt, Walt Meyer, Bill Armbrust, Bob Klinner, Jack Zhielke as well as Dick and me. We followed the rules and were always welcome. Our many visits to the camp encompassed all the things associated with being "up north": snowshoeing, walking through woods at fall time, waking early to the morning's sharp chill, the smell of wet wool and leather as we sat in front of the blazing fire, hamburgers and baked beans. Since Chick Fleming was older and more sophisticated he rarely joined us. I do remember, however, when he prepared a steak dinner. For this occasion the steaks were prepared over a bed of black ash wood coals. Good memories included many hours of sitting and talking in front of the fire, hearing rain patter on the roof or the whisper of pine needles falling on the roof. Not so pleasant memories but tolerable: the cold outdoor toilet, taking turns preparing meals, doing dishes, tending fire early on a cold morning.

One year our family had Christmas Eve dinner at the Ho Hum. Mother prepared turkey, dressing, sweet potatoes with steamed pudding dessert. Mr. and Mrs. Brandt, Frank and Laura, were our guests. A pleasant Currier and Ives type event.

Before Roylee and I were married we took a midnight snowshoe walk through the timber stand behind the cabin and almost got lost, silly but Roylee didn't realize the seriousness of our situation.

The tale of the Ho Hum may possibly seem monotonous and boring- boring, however I feel it helps to define life in mid-America small community. Lessons learned during outings there, by observation. Observation of the phases of the seasons, interpretations of nature, animal habits, tracks and trails, just the ability to commune with and enjoy the forest surroundings, all contribute to an enhanced quality of life. This along with the beginning and building of lifelong friendships really makes the Ho Hum experiences something very special.

Lake Esadore History

By Fred Pflughoeft

The first cottages built on the lake belonged to a group of families from Medford which formed a compound on the west shore. The names of these first group were Nystrum, Schief, and Urqhardt. Dr Esadore Nystrum is the person for whom the lake is named. This was sometime before 1900.

Lake Esadore was formed by a natural dam that closed the east end of the lake at a point near the present High View restaurant's picnic area. The original lake was at a considerably lower level at that time. I can remember my father showing me a submerged rock which had a cross chiseled into its top. This at one time designated a lot boundary. Sometime in the history, a wooden dam with spillway was placed on top of this natural dam raising the lake level about 18 inches. The remains of this early dam, several incline planks half buried in the sand, can still be seen underwater at this site. Subsequent to this, the present concrete dam with spillway was constructed at the east end of what is now Clear Lake. This dam flooded the creek exiting Lake Esadore on the east and formed Clear Lake, also raising Lake Esadore to its present level. The lake really doesn't have an inlet and is essentially spring fed.

Some years ago, I sounded the bottom and found several spots that were almost 60 feet deep. The present surface area of the lake is something over 50 acres satisfying the DNR requirement for allowing motor boats to make a wake thus allowing water skiing and tubing.

In 1931 our family friends, the Musselmans built a log cabin cottage. It was located in a row along the southeast shore. Shortly thereafter Father built our original place adjacent to the Musselmans. The floor support he built was very strong and he was kidded about building a platform for tractors. The walls were vertical logs flat on three sides and fitted smooth edge to smooth edge with the rounded surface outwards. It had two bedrooms, a living and dining space, a kitchen and a nice screened porch. When the cottage was completed, four families, my parents' good friends the

Flemmings, Ungrodts and Musselmans and of course our family had places along the south shore.

In those years, the 1930s, summer Sunday dinners were really a production. Hams from Musselman's bakery, baked beans, potato salad (several kinds), and cakes made by the best cooks in the state. All this food was laid out on two large porcelainized Fisk Company tire signs, probably three feet by six or seven feet, set up on saw horses and no paper plates. A large table of food. Outstanding.

Each Sunday Dick Muzzy, who was my boyhood chum, and I would get the task of driving four miles to Scharrschmidt's filling station and ice cream stand to pick up a gallon of delicious home-made ice cream. As drivers we were probably 12 to 14 years old, unbelievable. When it came time to wash dishes, Dick and I usually would crawl up on the backside of Muzzy's cottage roof and hide till clean up chores were completed.

First memories were of trying to get into the lake and swim as early as April. Burrrr. Early on there were two amusement establishments one on either end of the lake.

Spreen Resort located between Mud Lake and Lake Esadore boasted a dance hall and roller skating rink, as well as a bar room. On the lake, there were two diving boards. One was a 3 to 4 foot high board and the other was 7 to 8 feet high. There was also a roller coaster. Boards with small wheels were locked onto an incline track. These boards gave a quiet and swift ride down the track to shoot into the water. This was quite thrilling. Actually, it was an accident about to happen. Insurance?

Spreen Resort, as it was called, did have a motor powered launch which offered rides. A trip around the lake cost a dime. Keith Ungrodt was the resident boat pilot. Roylee says she remembers attending wedding dances at the Spreen's dance hall on Saturday nights during the summer.

At the other end of the lake, the east end, was the original High View Hall, a bar and dance hall. The High View was pretty much leveled in 1927-28 by a cyclone. I remember sitting with Mother riding out the storm at home while Father was called to the storm scene on a professional basis. The High View was later restored and I can remember the large ice house on the premises. Each time we were at the cottage it was necessary to go up to the ice house to pick up a block of ice for the ice box. We used to do this by boat – a real adventure. Each cottage had a pair of ice tongs. No electricity in those days. Actually for the first years at the cottage we relied upon gas and kerosene lamps as well as propane gas lights.

Other memories include Father taking me crappie fishing at a good hole in front of Benn's cottage. Actually many years later, I rediscovered this good hole and had several nice fishing times with Bill Armbrust.

At one time we had a lapstrake boat for which Mother fashioned a bed sheet sail and we kids made a valiant attempt at sailing. What fun! Before we were able to have a canoe, Father felt it was necessary for us to be able to swim comfortably across the lake. After Edith and I accomplished this, we received a green Old Town guide and trapper model canoe, complete with sailing rig, lee boards, rudder and sail. Chuck Fleming and the Muzzies also had sailing canoes which made for a lot of sailing fun.

One time Edith and I dumped while sailing the canoe, and after we got organized, here came Mother and Mrs. Ungrodt to our rescue rowing our cedar stripped double placed row boat. It was a gas to see the ladies rowing in perfect synchronization. Two elderly ladies on Coast Guard duty.

Every summer the Muzzies' cousins, the Rowes from Chicago, spent several weeks at the lake and again we kids had many good times.

The ever present raft kept us in the water practically all day. That first raft made of half round ties with a plank deck, it was a fore runner of the present raft. The present raft was a neighborhood effort and has been fun for big and small. At one time a trampoline was mounted on it. It also was great as a starting place for the young beginner water skiers.

One competitive game we played was a modified form of water polo. Using two row boats with small outboard motors and canoe paddles as mallets, the object was to drive a beach ball into a goal. One goal was the bay behind our present cottage, the other was the creek leading to Mud Lake.

Our greatest summer adventure was designing and constructing a diving helmet. We had a water heater tank cut to accommodate shoulder holes and a view port which held safety glass which Father cut for us. This was a real construction problem because of the flat view glass. The helmet was equipped with a garden hose and a double action tire pump. After we overcame the problem of the helmet wanting to seek an equilibrium at the water surface, we had a great time hard hat diving by exploring the bottom of the lake and so forth. Our answer to the equilibrium problem was adding iron bars at the front and back of the helmet thus increasing the weight and overcoming the tendency of the helmet to float.

The fireworks each Fourth of July consisted mostly of flares and Mount Vesuvius showers as well as pinwheels. Our group would combine our efforts and have a display at Flemming's pier and sanely and safely light them off at the same time watching other corners of the lake which had similar fireworks showings.

Mr. Musselman and Mrs. Fleming were sort of the coordinators for our inter-family activities. The

Musselmans, Ungrodts and we were in adjacent cottages but the Flemings were some distance down the lake. When Mr. Musselman wanted to communicate with Mrs. Fleming, they used a set of 8 inch megaphones and everyone on the lake knew our plan. This was of course before telephones and electricity.

Originally we entered our lot up the hill from Perkinstown Avenue. After Mother had her heart problem, Father checked into right of way access across the lots east of us and found that an easement did exist. After contacting the owners of the property, we drove in on what we called the bottom way. This apparently upset a Mr. Spreen who owned the lot just east of us. To impede our driving, he planted two trees – one in each tire rut of our new bottom way. He was adamant about not selling the lot to Father. Mrs. O'Malley, a great family friend, knew Spreen. She bought the lot and immediately sold it to Father. This way Mother could get to the cottage without having to navigate the steep hill on the back of our lot.

At one time the residents of Lake Esadore suffered a severe scare. Bank beaver had burrowed holes in the side approaches to the dam. Before the lake had drained out, all the home owners got together and made hasty repairs which have endured to the present. It is possible that the beaver were trapped and moved. Mr. Harry Hosford who was the local game warden was a friend of our parents' group.

From time to time, in periods of drought, the lake level would drop to a point where 3 to 4 feet of beach was uncovered. Fortunately, this was only temporary and generally the lake has kept its level. As I mentioned, the lake is essentially spring fed and nature has been very kind. Every spring the lake is back to its maximum level with water going over the spillway at the dam. Most always the water quality appears good, although I have some concern about the bacterial count.

Father always liked the point which was part of the lot we acquired from Mr. Spreen. It was Father's wish to build another cottage there. The original plat showed the point as being an island. During our ownership, it was not actually an island. It was attached to the rest of the lot by a swampy area. As a matter of fact when we were young, Dick Muzzy, Don Urquhardt and I imagined digging a channel through this area and actually creating an island. Needless to say we never did it. Just like De Lesseps on the Panama Canal.

For many years we had a boat house on the west end of this isthmus. The boat house is long gone.

The central area of the point where our cottage now stands was about three feet above the usual lake level. There was evidence of early campfires having been burned here. Interesting to speculate, since this is one of the areas that Marquette had explored early on. It really was a scenic spot.

Father built the cottage in about 1952-53. It has two bedrooms with double bunks, kitchen, large living room, heated with a fireplace and a porch on the north side. Father did a lot of the inside finishing work after the roof was on and the walls completed. He did things like panel the ceiling and the innovation of double bunk beds and room partitions.

After we all became established and had family time, Dick and Rachel's families and our gang spent many glorious summers at the lake. One of the very memorable experiences was our introduction to water skiing. Our first attempt was with Dick and Scott Loucks and me, we used our wooden cedar stripped row boat. Mother would rent a heavier motor for us and we fashioned the tow rope from cotton clothes line. This was a weak plan. We would just about get up on the skis and the rope would break and when the boat driver cut the speed of the motor the stern wave would almost swamp the boat coming over the transom. After some time we worked it out and everyone learned to ski. The kids especially became excellent skiers. Jane, Martha, John and all the Loucks and Muzzy kids. Bill Scharrschmidt had a heavier rig and we now had an aluminum boat with a faithful Mercury engine. With these two units, the kids really got in a lot of skiing. Even the adults had a chance to ski. We formed the Erodase Ski Club, that is Esadore spelt backwards. As members of the ski club, the kids had to put on a performance from time to time and these performances were enjoyed by all. It was lots of fun. Some person, I think it may have been Bowen from across the lake, had a fairly heavy inboard outboard ski boat and he would pull six of our kids each skiing on one ski. It was quite a performance and exhilarating for the children.

The standing joke to this day is that the last two times I skied the boat ran out of gas at the far end of the lake and I had to swim home while the boat was rowed home. Since it appeared that I jinxed skiing, I retired for the good of the Club.

Nancy's husband, Dick, and Bill bought a boat called the Lark. This is a whole other story.

For years Father and his buddies would play cards every Monday rotating cottages, Mickler's, Dodsworth's, Hirsch's and ours. The wives apparently got up in arms about the cottages not being properly cleaned after these sessions and the persistence of the smell of cigar smoke, and in deference, the men purchased a farm house adjacent to the lake, removed all the first floor partitions and installed a refrigerator, stove and several card tables. No dishwasher, since the losing card players washed the dishes. The Monday Club, as it was called, did have a good well and was a major source of drinking water. Prior to this, most of the water was carried from the town of Medford.

Sometime along the line we finally acquired a real sailboat, the sunfish. It was relaxing and fun to have either Jane, Martha or John take Roylee and me for a sail. The Muzzies soon had a sunfish also. This made for a little good natured competition.

Weekends at the cottage were a wonderful chance for Roylee and me to recharge, especially in those years that we lived quite close in Markesan. Swimming, hiking and just sitting, sometimes all by ourselves. Ah, fond memories.

I think we really usurped the cottage during those summers and the Boyles didn't get much use of it. I do feel rather guilty about this, however lately they have been using it more frequently which is great. We really had hoped the Boyles would join us for cottage vacations just as the Muzzy families got together.

The past memories and present times are wonderful. One of the traditions over the years is a Ross family reunion. Every second year, alternating with a visit to Eloise's home in Virginia, Illinois, we get together at the cottage. We have had as many as 30 persons for the reunion held on the 4th of

July week. Lots of people. Lots of fun. Water sports, golf, food, and so forth, and usually a project, paint, tree removal, tear down a shed and so forth. Noth's cottage across the bay and several tents act as additional housing.

One memorable project was the restoration of John's hydroplane. Time had been hard on the boat so the cousins spent the week fully restoring the boat until it was runnable. It really had a workout after they got it fixed, but unfortunately, the hydroplane now has passed.

The coincidence of the Ross reunion and the lake association's annual meeting has netted the association several memberships from the St. Louis area. This makes for our group taking part in social activities of the meeting, balloon toss, frog jump and so forth. For really complete coverage of the Ross reunion I highly recommend a scrapbook that Sara and Joanne have compiled.

Father made three signs for the cottage which explain it all. The first one which hung in a tree says "Unser Schloss" which translates to "Our Castle". The two indoor signs were more philosophical. "Arger dich nicht" which literally translated means "aggravate yourself not", a good thought. And in English a sign, "For the young folks, we leave a memory." All really poignant.

My hope is that the present cottage can remain in the family for many years and that the children can all have as much fun as we did. Rachel, Peter and Lauren and Dana seem to be taken to the atmosphere and routine of lake living. I hope that Amy will have a chance to become acquainted with the cottage under the best of circumstances.

For years, it was believed that we couldn't find water in this area, and there wasn't a practical method to deal with the sewage problem. We feel that this has been taken care of, and with our new space heater, visits to the cottage are much more comfortable.

There are a thousand pictures of tender moments. Jane reading in the hammock on the raft with Wolfgang snoozing next to the hammock. Martha and Nacy Musselman paddling along in a large truck inner tube trailing along behind a small tube carrying their lunch. John cutting wood with a chain saw on his property on the corner of E & M.

Roylee hunkered down over the steering wheel of John's hydroplane zipping around the lake. The time Jack Boyle and I were fishing. Jack hooked into a lunker and in landing it he stepped out of the canoe into the lake (waist deep) but did land a nice size bass. Great, great, great! What more can I say!

Bill has been preserving the lawn by use of a resilient sod from the golf course.

Dick, Nancy, and Martha worked hard to restore the canoe to mint condition. A thing to behold.

Mary (our bat control person), Martha and Bill have accepted the chore of up keep and I am sure that the cottage will be a source of fun and joy for all members of the family.

Main Street, Medford, Wisconsin – A Memory

Main Street, Medford, WI has its root opposite the Carnegie Library on Perkins Street. Carnegie Foundation supported free libraries in many American small towns. They were constructed following an attractive architectural design in the 1920's. Main Street extends northward about one mile to the present day library *(Francis L. Simek Memorial Library built???? about 10 years before her death)*. Early on car-parking was at an angle to the street. As cars became more frequent and larger, they caused consternation for drivers. The change to parallel parking didn't completely relieve the frustrations.

On the east side, the first of only a few residences on Main Street, was the Suits family home, now replaced by an apartment complex. Originally the next building north of the Suits home was the parsonage for a Unitarian church that had a large gymnasium adjacent to the church. The gym was open to the young men/boys of Medford on

Saturday mornings until the young men & boys became too rambunctious and broke up the tables and chairs in the gym. This nefarious action brought the Sat morning gym use to a halt.

On a hill just behind the gym was a large vacant area. It had remained empty for some time after the hotel that had occupied the top of the hill burned *(before Daddy's memory)*. This allowed for good sledding in the winter. Presently this area is occupied by an automotive business.

Next north building is the U.S. Post Office building *(USPS is currently 1 block west of Main Street just south of Hwy 64)*. The construction of the Post Office building is an interesting story of community effectiveness. Medford as it grew needed a better Postal Service building. This was the period referred to as the New Deal Era (1930s). A Medford native son working in Washington D.C. knew that they were due for a new postal building of this period of postal expansion. He further advised his Medford friends that if they approached the construction of a new Post Office properly (meaning slow acceptance of the project) the town was in line for a more classy building. Result being Medford did receive an efficient new Post Office of attractive architectural style. This accounts for the relatively nice building filling out the first block of Main Street's east side.

The block ends with a short street proceeding up the hill to the County Court House block. The County Court House is an early American building. The lawn around the building had 48 large spruce trees (one for each state) and a statue of an American Dough boy.

This short street was occupied on the south side by a tavern. On the north side coming down the hill was the Pflughoeft Hartwig Funeral Home. The next building was originally the Telephone office; later occupied by the Hudson Bay Trading Post and a dry cleaning establishment on the corner shared with Main Street. It was unusual to have a Hudson's Bay property in a small town, however the large number of fox and mik ranches in the Medford area most likely accounted for the presence of a fur company post.

The west side of Main Street starting from the library was mostly vacant. It did include a beer company building and the Emmons Paint Store which was on the corner.

At one time a building in this area was vacant when Martha and her friend *(Cathy Osenga)* rented it for a summer *(1970)* to sell craft things. Their store was called the Appleknocker. *For the first few days of its existence, it had a beautiful apple-shaped, red, wooden sign made by Pat Loucks (of the Musselman family) but the sign was stolen. There is a rumor that Ann Klinner knows who did it and possibly where the sign is now?*

To proceed northward, along the east side of Main Street was the cleaning company mentioned previously. Next was a small grocery store, property of Mr. E. E. Grubber. He was a kindly old man who worried a lot. This personality qualified him to be the recipient of practical jokes. One of the favourite jokes perpetrated by the adjacent merchants was to make footprints in a new snow up to his store early in the morning. This caused him to question himself "Why did they come so early?" Consequently he arrived at his store ½ hour earlier the next few mornings but no customer.

The next building proceeding north was Father's (Werner Pflughoeft) furniture store. Next to that a boutique that also sold notions. The claim to fame for this establishment was the words of a lady celebrated for her colourful speech. One of her quotes on the price of a crucifix was "My, but that little devil is expensive."

Armbrust's Meat Market was *(and still is!)* next and then a bakery which had a spectacular fire bringing out all the citizens – a night time fire. I don't remember the year, but I do remember that Father rolled me out early in the morning to see the spectacle. The fire damage was limited to the bakery building – a plus grade for the local volunteer fire brigade.

The Ideal Café, City Hotel and Benn's Drugstore, the original Post Office building and then Angel Flight. The proprietor of the drugstore was August Benn. August fell victim to one of the practical jokes by his adjacent merchant friends. In very cavalier way, the merchants, if they saw one of their friends come into their establishment, would shout out "Close the door". Poor myopic August wanted to be as cavalier aas the other merchants. He took up the same challenge. The only problem being that he didn't recognise who was entering his store – cried out the challenge "Close the door!" The unfamiliar voice replied, "Yes, sir, and from the outside", click. Poor Mr Benn.

There was a passage between the very old Post Office and the next structure to the north. This led to the Angel Flight, a flight of stairs which was a fairly strenuous climb to 2nd Street.

To bring up the west side of Main Street, the corner building was the headquarters of the Taylor County Newspaper called the Star News. It had a linotype machine in the front window and frequently drew spectators. Early on a cobbler had a small shop next to the street. He worked at his bench which was street level behind a plate glas window. It was reported that a humorous event took place here. One day while the cobbler was working at his bench, a car jumped the curb, breaking the window in front of the cobbler. He was not injured but it was reported that his first words were, "If you had waited a minute, I would have opened the door."

Mose Poiere's store – home appliances – was next. An ice cream store followed and then a big barber shop. Gpa Schief was the head barber and put 2 sons through dental school with profits from the shop. The last business of this side of Main Street before a short east-west side street which went to the Medford Clinic, was Mayor Leupke's completely stocked hardware store. Across this short street was the National Bank building which foundered in the Great Depression. The building was taken over by the State Bank – a more conservative enterprise which survived the depression. (Became Mid-Wisconsin where Martha works now)

Crossing back to the east side of Main Street, the first building after Angel Flight was the old State Bank building which had morphed into a hardware store. Suits Drugstore, a small tavern, Schmidt the Clothes man, then three big store fronts which held Newburg's men's and women's clothing, another store selling notions (which is now part of the Ben Franklin/St Vinnie's frontage), a meat market and then Musselman's bakery and grocery store. One of Musselman's pranks took place in his store: There were tables and chairs where fellows frequently met for coffee& bakery. When they sat down, Mr Musselman inquired, "Do you smell something? I do. Look at your shoes to see if you stepped in some dog do." Unbeknownst to the group, Mr

M had put some ginger cookie dough on his shoe and said, "Look, I do". He touched it with his finger and put it to his mouth and said, "Sure enough". This broke up the meeting.

The next building was the Avon Theater. This was the Blaksley enterprise. People went early to be intrigue by the theatre ceiling which had floating clouds and sparkling stars prior to lights out for the movie. *(Clouds/stars projected onto the ceiling- I remember seeing this once)*

A small jewelry store was next. The parents of every child purchased a mechanical pencil and fountain pen set for their proud High School graduates. Heimerl's, a progressive five and dime store, was followed by a well stocked grocery store. Another barber shop, a plumbing establishment and dry goods store completed the east of Main. The cross street was Broadway. A busy east-west thoroughfare – Hwy 64.

Back on the west side of Main Street, there were several vacant lots north of the bank building. A cigar store, a lawyers office and the Keefe furniture store. Several more vacant lots and a grain elevator ended the west side at Hwy 64.

North of Hwy 64, both sides were light industry. A fishing lure factory. Pontiac automobile dealer, petroleum tanks, a metal salvage establishment which unbeknownst to them supplied the extra weight metal bars fastened to the diving helmet.

In the original time the pea canning factory capped the north end of Main Street. Today the new city library replaces the canning factory as the north end of Main Street. *Shirley Lemke – librarian – described the day that the junior high students were given the afternoon off from classes to carry armfuls of books from the old Carnegie Library to the new library building – I can't remember which year but I think Rachel Klinner was one of the students.)*

To the northwest of the library is the recently dedicated memorial wall and flag display to military veterans.

F. A. Pflughoeft

January 2011

(italicised additions by J Plowman)

The Diving Helmet Story

By Fred Pflughoeft written 2000-2001

The time of this adventure was the summer of 1941. The Musselmans had replaced their water heater. Dick reclaimed the steel tank and had great plans. Together with a neighbor, and fellow engineering student at the University of Wisconsin, Don Urquhardt, they designed an alternative use for the steel tank, a "diving helmet".

I have a suspicion that I was included in the project as an aid for finances.

Dick and Don had an understanding of the physics of holding air accessible to a submerged person. They designed the concept of supplying air to someone walking below the surface of the water. With the plan in mind it was necessary to arrange for its execution.

An employee in the Strebig garage in Medford came to our rescue. It was obvious that some alterations would be necessary to convert the steel tank into a diving helmet. The tank had to be cut to a proper length and cutouts to accommodate the shoulders. This was relatively simple. Construction of a view port was a little more serious. The tank was altered to allow a view port to project from the front curved surface. The projected front surface also required a flat flange about 1 ½ inches wide surrounding the opening to which a transparent glass window could be attached. A narrow metal frame surrounding the outer edge of the glass and help to retain it was required. It was also necessary to drill and tap a number of bolt holes around the edge to hold the components (the metal frame, the glass and the flat flange surrounding the opening of the port) together as a sealed unit.

The garage employee, Harold Pernsteiner, with his welding skills was able to accomplish these requirements.

The diving helmet was taking shape. It was decided to use a flat laminated piece of automobile windshield for the viewing port. This presented a chore. Since Father, as a sort of hobby, framed pictures at the furniture store, he was called upon to cut the glass to its proper size. Both sides of the windshield were scribed and cut, however, cutting the celluloid laminate between the layers of glass presented a problem. Since the celluloid layer had a greater coefficient of expansion than the glass, the entire section was submerged in super hot water. The heat softened the celluloid and caused it to expand sufficiently so a thin sharp blade could be inserted to cut the celluloid to the proper shape. The view port glass was layered with automotive gasket material and then bolted into place.

The sharp lower edge of the helmet was covered with a section of heavy bicycle tire held in place by means of light weight machine bolts around the entire periphery.

A section of garden hose was responsible to carry air from the surface to the submerged helmet. A double action manual tire pump was the source of the air. This type of pump expelled air on both upward and down strokes, which was necessary to insure a constant supply of air in the helmet. The air pressure was sufficient to maintain the water level inside the helmet at just slightly above the highest point of the shoulder cutouts. Harold also fabricated an attachment, with a tire valve incorporated, to connect the pump to the garden hose, "life line", another safety measure.

To preclude pulling stress on the hose a rope was used to aid lowering and raising the helmet.

At this point a trial "dive" was attempted. The Medford mill pond at an area near the Lindow gas storage tank was selected. I'm quite sure Dick initiated the diving helmet. This trial met with frustration. As Dick walked out into the deep water the tank sought a level with its top slightly above the water surface, and as Dick proceeded to deeper water he walked right out from under the helmet. The buoyancy of the water combined with the included air allowed the helmet to sink only so far. We vetoed using straps to hold the helmet to the diver. Obviously more weight was required to overcome the undesired amount of buoyancy.

We located an iron bar of proper dimensions at the salvage yard. That evening after dark as the three of us walked abreast through the salvage yard the object of our search just happened to cling to our hands.

The Musselman basement was the venue for our next task. The bar was cut into six lengths by manual hack saw. Bolt holes were made in each length of the bar and corresponding holes in the helmet surface by means of a small electric drill. A hot, dirty, tiresome job which lasted into the early morning. Rather than go home I slept on Musselman's second floor porch.

Here I must digress. Early the next morning (Sunday) it was necessary to take the car home so my parents could go to church. On the way I passed one of the Wicker twins as she was walking to church. I offered her a ride and as she sat in the car her knees were slightly exposed. When I related this to Dick, he said he would have put his hand on her knee. My reply was, "I wouldn't do that and besides my hands were blistered and dirty from the previous night's work."

With the added weight in place, Flemming's pier on Lake Esadore was the next site for a dive. The solid diving board made a good platform for the pumper and the water here was rather deep. The added weight tipped the balance and the helmet stayed in place on the diver's shoulders as he walked into the water.

We carried on diving at Flemming's and also at Spreen's Resort, also on Lake Esadore, where the water was deeper. Curious blue gills and sunfish were the most exciting things viewed while submerged. However, quite exciting was the first time you realized the water level in the helmet was slowly raising above your chin, indicating the pumpers were failing in their job. After that experience no one would venture down if Dick was manning the pump.

Harold, a good friend at the garage also took care of other little problems we kids might have with the family car, scratches, dings, etc. One of the hairy incidents he helped us with augers for me to tell this story.

It all started with a wiener roast on a warm summer night. Dick and Rachel, Bill Armbrust and a girl friend, my sister Edith and two cousins Almarlyn and Margey and I drove up to North Twin Lake, had a pleasant picnic and when it came time to return home it was decided that Bill Armbrust and his girl friend, Dick and Almarlyn would drive home in my Father's car. It had a radio and it made for a more romantic drive through the forest. The rest of us all piled into Bill's open roadster and I drove them home. Plans called for us to meet later at Musselman's home in Medford. While we were waiting for them to return it became very late and we began to worry a little. What to tell parents about our cousin arriving home so late. About this time the tow truck from Strebig's garage went by in the direction of the area that our tardy friends should be. This now was cause for alarm. A check with the garage told us that Dick's group had become stuck in a forest lane "sink hole" and needed a tow truck. They must have walked three miles to a telephone to call in the distress. Wow!

I dropped off the rest of our group of the picnickers and waited at the garage. When the errant fellows arrived it was apparent they had been in a mud hole. The mud in the car extended to about 5 inches above the floor. The car was to be used to carry mourners at a funeral the next morning. Two problems: smuggle Almarlyn into the house and clean up the car.

With Harold's help Dick, Bill and I washed and desmelled the messy car. It can be laughed about now, but it was pretty serious at the time, and many thanks to Harold.

The diving helmet seemed to disappear, the war and jobs and families took precedent. The summer of 2000 I asked Dr. Walther Meyer of Medford, one of our gang, if he had any idea where the helmet might be. His reply was, "It may be in the attic of my garage." It was there and Walt delivered it to the cottage on July 4, 2000. This certainly recalled memories.

Extracts of 'The Dive' by W. Peter Scotland in Soundings – journal of Wisconsin Marine Historical Society, Volume 46, No. 4, Winter 2006

'On August 26th of this last summer I had the unique privilege of being part of a dive using two historically significant diving helmets. The first helmet, owned by WMHS member Fred Pflughoeft, is significant because it is a sixty-five year old version of the early prototypes used to develop modern diving helmets.....

'The event took place on the shore of Lake Michigan, in South Shore Park, on the south side of Milwaukee.....

'In the spring while I was doing some work at the library, Fred Pflughoeft, knowing my interest in diving, came to me and told me a fascinating story of how he and three of his friends had built a diving helmet years ago. It had recently been found by a relative, under some rubble, in a building used for storage. Here is Fred's description of the helmet:

'"The homemade helmet was designed and constructed in 1941 by four lads in Medford, Wi. It was used on a small inland lake for recreation only. The helmet was constructed from a discarded water heater storage tank. Air was supplied by a hand pump and a garden hose. There was no means of securing the helmet to the diver and it was necessary for the diver to maintain an upright position while walking submerged. In the design, because of buoyancy, it was necessary to fasten additional weights to the front and back of the helmet. Inside pressure kept the water level about chin high."

'After telling me this story I suggested he bring the helmet to Milwaukee and I would restore it for him as best I could and try diving in it. (Genius!) About a month later Fred and his wife, Roylee, show up with the helmet and I went to lift it out of the trunk of their car to carry into my house and the thought struck me that this baby must have been REAL buoyant underwater. It weighed about ninety pounds! After staggering into my basement with it and later talking to Fred and Roylee, we decided that since there were no moving parts on it and to keep the historical integrity intact no restoration would be undertaken.

'In the photo of Fred's helmet you can see the rivets of the old storage tank and the cast steel weights that were added to both the front and back to negate its buoyancy. The air entered through the piping on the top and exited out the open bottom. The face plate was made from a car window. The diameter of the tank was thirteen inches and the height was thirty-four inches including the piping.

'Fred couldn't remember where the idea and design inspiration for the helmet had come from, but some helpful research by [WMHS workers] turned up two articles in a magazine called Modern Mechanic. The first was in the January 1932 issue and was titled BUILD A DIVING HELMET FROM A WATER HEATER, no kidding, and the second was from the June 1933 edition called BUILD YOUR OWN DIVING HELMET. Obviously the libel laws were less stringent in those days, but I think that these articles might have influenced the construction of this helmet.....

'I made my ...dive ...in Fred's helmet. With my interest in diving history I felt honored to dive this helmet built by Fred and his buddies back in 1941. The principles of diving are fairly simple, so I had no apprehension donning this basic, early type model of diving gear. The helmet worked fine and just as Fred said, the air pressure kept the water at about chin level with the excess air exhausting through the bottom of the helmet. The only work I did to the helmet was to put a valve on the air supply line, which is visible in the photographs.

'This type of helmet doesn't get attached to either the diver or his suit, but just sits on his shoulders. The main drawback to this was if the diver bends over the helmet had a tendency to slip off his head thus leaving the diver in a slight predicament. Fortunately for divers, the development of helmets has progressed.'

The diving helmet is on exhibit at the Taylor County Historical Society and Museum in Medford, Wisconsin.

Summer 1939

Washington DC and East

By Fred A. Pflughoeft

This "history" is being written as a result of a promise to Roylee that someday I would tell the story of one of my experiences. It is not in anyway meant to be boastful but rather the documentation of an interesting and fun event. The event concerns four high school kids who turned a wish into a happening. The wish to see part of our country by means of a road trip.

Since we all were markedly influenced by our high school Civics teacher Mr. Guy D'Rozio, it followed that the trip should be toward our National Capital. The students considered Guy a good teacher and a nice person. Through the years we have visited with Guy, and each time we saw him, he would relate his pleasant business experiences as a young married buying furniture from Father. And, also since our English teacher had just moved to Washington with her newly elected United States Senator father,

Washington, DC was our principal destination. Winifred (Fritzi) Wiley was our vivacious and patriotic English teacher. Her most memorable assignment was to learn and memorize the second stanza of the Star Spangled Banner.

The genesis of this adventure began on a spring evening when three of my high school buddies drove into our yard and asked me if I would like to join them in a summer trip to take place after school recessed. This was quite a thrill to me and I am sure my reaction was probably anything but as pleased and surprised as I really felt. The three fellows were Bob Klinner, Dick Musselman, and Don Urquhardt; all seniors about to graduate – I was one year their junior. Bob had a 28 model Chevrolet sedan which he used in commuting to school. This is the car we would use.

After coming back down to earth, I of course replied "yes, when do we start!" It wasn't quite that easy. There was no doubt about the three of them graduating, so on to the planning. The logistics required by this undertaking were quite a chore. A shelter was needed for camping, folding cots, sleeping bags, cooking utensils, a camp stove, and canned food. What kind of food, how much and also funds, funds for fresh food, emergencies, etc. were considered.

All the articles had to be collected, along with clothing for three weeks, not only collected but organized to fit into a trunk that fit on the back of Bob's car. Along with that was the decision of which route, destinations, time to be spent at stops enroute, etc. What a big order of organization for four kids.

Dick had an aunt and uncle in New Jersey. It would be the place to stay and make arrangements to visit the 1939 New York World's Fair as well as a tour of New York City. A friend of our Father's heard about the proposed experience (undoubtedly the entire town new about it) and said a trip to the East Coast would be incomplete without a stop at the United States military installation at Havre de Grace, Maryland – Aberdeen Proving Grounds. It just happened that this person (Vince Hirsch) had a brother that was a Major stationed there and would be happy to have us visit. Great! What a testimony for good friends in a small town.

Our plans and organization progressed. Destinations were Washington, DC, Aberdeen Proving Grounds, New York City and the fair in Flushing Meadows. All equipment, food, and clothes were stowed in the trunk and Dick's Dad sent along a large duck decoy bag which could be tied to the top of the car to be used for any overflow.

The route decided upon was highway 41 south to Cross Country 30, the Pennsylvania Turnpike on down to Washington. A side trip to Havre de Grace in Northeastern Maryland, Gettysburg, Pennsylvania, onto Plainfield, New Jersey where Dick's relatives the Conrad family lived. After that north to Albany, west across the top of the Finger Lakes and onto Niagara Falls. A duck into Ontario and through the state of Michigan to Ludington, a ride on the Lake Michigan ferry and then home.

What an undertaking. Could it be done? Of course it could and with the blessings of our parents. Surely each of our Mothers harbored the ubiquitous reservations but were gracious enough not to mention them.

Mr. Klinner was in accounting and insurance. Dick's father was a baker and had a grocery store and Mr. Urquhardt was an attorney. Each in their own way supported us.

I must add an important aside at this point. Bob was a very conservative high school student and the most off colored epithet he would utter was a seldom "you A hole," pretty conservative for a young man, more about this later.

We started very early in the morning since we had to make the most of each travel day. Our average speed was rather slow especially when compared to today's highway travel.

Our beginning was uneventful and our first day rations probably consisted of nice box lunches prepared by our Mothers. After this, we had to cook for ourselves.

Ft Wayne, Indiana, was our first stop in the second day and it is rather worth mentioning. In Ft Wayne, the Lincoln Highway (30) passed along one side of a typical Midwestern town square. This prompted us to stop for a rest from driving and we each rested in our own way. The most interesting of the rests was reported by Don. He sat on a public bench in the square and struck up a conversation with several of the "old timers" and reported an interesting insight from his talks. Mostly the subjects were national politics and the plight of the Midwestern farmer. This was interesting since one of our destinations was a visit with a political figure. A Midwestern U. S. Senator, Winifred's father.

The trip continued smoothly except that Don had a heavy foot and it seemed to us that he had in mind to test one of the runaway truck exits on the Pennsylvania Turnpike. Consequently he was the first of the three of us to be dubbed with the expletive "you A hole". Eventually each of us was likewise honored. My idiosyncrasy was hurrying up to a red light and dawdling slowly through a green one. I have an explanation for this.

Our first stop after arriving in Washington was to contact Fritzi (Winifred) in the Senator's office. She was happy to see us and loaded us down with admission passes to all the interesting venues. The F.B I., Treasury Department, Capitol Building, White House and many more, all part of the really first class treatment she had planned for us. Included was an evening boat ride on the Potomac River. Also along on the trip was her future husband Harold Wilde. Even four crass high school boys realized that we were privy to a budding romance. Winifred and Harold kept out tent site at the Tidal Basin Campground well supplied with ice cream and cookies. Something really appreciated by hungry boys.

Senator Wiley took us to lunch in the Senate Dining Room and introduced us to the subterranean railroad system that connected the several office buildings to the Capitol. We fellows made good use of this little gem. At lunch the Senator introduced us to some very heavy (prestigious) personages, our introduction to the world of international politics. Michigan's Senator Arthur Van Den Berg was our connection to six degrees of separation.

We were fortunate to see a parade in honor of the King and Queen of England and, of course, Franklin and Eleanor were also present. We climbed the Washington Monument, visited the Lincoln Memorial and the Nation's Capitol Building, rode out to Arlington Cemetery and saw the Tomb of the Unknown Soldier, then drove to Mount Vernon. What an impressive place with rolling lawns, stark white buildings and the family crypt.

What a really exciting experience for four small town boys. We were indebted to our English teacher for so much of it. Starting to feel sort of cosmopolitan, we reported to the United States Military testing facility, the Aberdeen Proving Grounds near Havre de Grace, Maryland. We drove up to the sentry on duty at the entrance gate and asked for Major Hirsch. In no time at all he appeared and presently installed us in his officers' quarters home. We really didn't consider his poor wife but she was an absolutely great sport. She fed us and the Major gave us an excellent tour of the base, the chance to view testing of artillery pieces and trial firing of all sorts and types of ammunition. In the back of my mind it seems we presented Mrs. Hirsch with a toaster when we left. Hopefully we did do something. It is interesting to note that many years later after World War II, Roylee and I had the opportunity to visit several times with returned prisoner of war Colonel Hirsch and his wife at the Hirsch Cottage on Lake Esadore. The visits were pleasant and most enlightening.

On to Gettysburg and surely we had some serious thoughts about what happened there.

Our next experience started when we "dropped in" on the Conrads at Plainfield, New Jersey. The family had four children and they succeeded to fit us in just great. Mr. Conrad took us on a tour of New York City including Radio City Music Hall, Empire State Building, Times Square, the Bowery and a Hudson River ferry ride. The family included us in a Sunday picnic to Barnegat Beach. It was a very nice fun day. A full day's trip to the 1939 Worlds Fair, which we arranged for ourselves and included several of the Conrad kids, rounded out our stay at Plainfield. A memory. Billy Rose's water spectacular at the fair was outstanding.

Here is about the midpoint in our trip. It was time to head home. We drove up the Storm King Highway past West Point Military Academy and Bear Mountain and then headed west along the Erie Canal.

At Skaneateles our one disappointing moment caught up with us and it really wasn't so serious. The 28 Chevy had a propensity for rear axle breakage. This happened on Dick's watch for driving and he inducted himself immediately into the A hole society. It took about a half a day for the mechanical repairs. I can't remember, or not for sure, but I think we had a restaurant lunch meal at Krebs while waiting. It seems to me that the name of the restaurant was suggested by Mrs. Fleming a friend of our parents. Roylee has fond memories of Krebs. She visited it with her mother on a family trip through New York State. Many years later, Roylee and I again looked up the restaurant while on a visit to the Finger Lakes area. It still was in existence. Actually the wait for car repairs wasn't all bad. It gave us a chance to visit the city beach.

After the delay, it was on to Niagara Falls. We visited the Falls at night. I remember being immensely impressed – actually awed.

When we crossed into Ontario, the Customs officer noted the large decoy bag tied to the top of the car and asked what it contained. Some on quipped "dirty clothes" and the official just said "Oh, you lazy kids."

Our experiences were coming to an end. The last one consisted of a ferry ride from Ludington, Michigan, to Kewaunee, Wisconsin. We picked an especially bad day for our first boat crossing. It was cold and wet and very rough. I don't know about the other fellows but sea sickness caught up with me on that trip.

All ended well. We had a three week life time experience full of good fun and memories. No conflicts or words in anger. Following the trip we remained fast friends.

Don, an Air Force pilot, was a casualty of World War II. Dick, an inveterate kidder and friend, passed away much too young.

It is possible that in telling this history some things were inadvertently omitted or embellished. Bob and I will have to work this out.

Membership in the A Hole Club, which was later extended to include Bill and Walt, was for life time. When exchanging written correspondence, the letter would either begin or end with the symbol [captital A in a circle] and subsequently when meeting each other, "A hole" was part of the greeting.

written? when? (1940 trip was written about in 1993) (after Dick's death)

Bill Armbrust's car before alterations for trip.
Walt Meyer   Bill (driving)
     FAP   Reuben Hackbarth

and after
          Reuben H.   Bill (driving)
Walt Meyer   FAP

Our Trip - 1940

Historian Fred Pflughoeft 1993

In the past few years, the impermanence of "Oral History" has become impressed on Roylee and me. Numerous times, we have regretted the fact that we have neglected to document history as told by family members over the years.

At Roylee's suggestion, I will relate an early experience; the story of a car trip which Roylee and I feel should be preserved. An event that took its beginning as a high school dream, made possible when Bill Armbrust's parents gave him a Model A Ford Roadster.

The car was a little beauty with a manual folding top, dual side mount spare wheels with rear view mirrors strapped in place on top of each spare wheel. The mechanics of this four cylinder engine was relatively uncomplicated and gas mileage was outstanding.

Since transportation appeared to be solved, we started early in our Senior year of high school to plan a trip. Mexico City seemed a logical destination especially after reading the exciting stories of the author Richard Haliburton.

Practicing our pidgin Spanish was great fun even during football practice. Coach Koenig good naturedly chided us about our errant pronunciation of important words such as "altos".

Inquiries into the practical aspects of travel in Mexico soon convinced us that we should change our destination and a circle tour to the Pacific coast seemed much more reasonable.

The "we" mentioned above consisted of Bill Armbrust, Ruben Hackbarth and Walt Meyer and, of course, me. Bill lived across the street from me. He and I were boyhood chums. Bill's father was a master butcher and the proprietor of our local meat market and his mother was really good about taking us fishing before we were old enough to ride our bikes on the highway. Ruben lived near the high school. His father was an engineer at Hurd's, a sash and door factory in Medford; his mother frequently had a cookie supply for us when we visited Ruben to build model airplanes. Walter Meyer's father was an entrepreneur, owner of the local radio station and also into politics. Walt's mother, Irma, was always encouraging us to have a good time.

During the late winter and early spring months of our senior year in high school, plans took shape. A route and points to be visited were decided upon, food, sleeping facilities and funds were discussed and plans finalized. Since I had been on a similar type trip the previous summer with three other fellows, it followed that I was the logical candidate for trip treasurer. In preparation for my handling of the funds, my father made a deerskin money belt for me. The belt was to be worn under my shirt.

It was necessary to make some modifications to Bill's car. A box to hold food was fixed to one running board. The other running board was equipped to carry a large duffel with tent, blankets, and folding canvas army cots. A large trunk box, for holding our clothes, was strapped to the rear foldable trunk rack. Needless to say, four high school lads didn't require large quantities of clothing. One trunk was sufficient.

The car had no cover over the rumble seat; something innovative was necessary to protect the occupants of the back seat from rain and possibly snow. A canvas canopy stretched over a collapsible frame was designed to cope with inclement weather.

With these modifications and the addition of a dish pan, a canteen, a water bag and a portable camp stove, the roadster was almost ready to go. And so were we with the blessings of our parents.

Over the years, people have asked the question: "Would you allow your children to make a trip like this planned by four high school lads?" My answer must be that for many reasons it's a different world out there with different concerns.

After 1940 Spring Graduation, we filled the food box with cans of beans, beef stew and a variety of soups. Each of the four of us anted up $40 for the kitty.

We were ready to start on our adventure.

A vision of the car was something reminiscent of the Joad family in Steinbeck's book "The Grapes of Wrath".

The beginning of the trip is rather vague in my mind. Obviously we started west through Minnesota.

An extremely hot day in South Dakota is my first real memory. Since the sun was intense and riding with the top down we duly protected our faces and arms with suntan lotion. Driving on, we encountered road work and the detour on a gravel road was very dusty. When we stopped to make camp that evening, it was amusing to see our dust encrusted faces and arms. A campground in Pierre offered us a chance to shower and clean up so we could be acceptable campers.

The Badlands State Park of South Dakota was next on our itinerary and after the Badlands, the Black Hills were delightfully green and refreshing by comparison. The tree covered hills were a welcome sight, also the Borglum sculptures, the Needles section and Sylvan Lake were very impressive. The sculpture of the presidents rated a very precarious stop in one of the highway tunnels so properly framed photographs could be made.

From the Black Hills, we continued west through eastern Wyoming to the Big Horn Mountains. Here a cold rain with some flakes of snow tested our improvised weather protection. Needless to say, when we arrived at Buffalo, we were wet and cold. Here we rented the first, of only four, motel accommodations used during the entire trip. The kitchen stove in the inexpensive housekeeping motel-cabin was used to help us dry out.

With dry clothes and a good night's sleep, we were ready the next day to continue on into the Big Horn Mountain country.

With our stored up energy, we climbed a mountain side. I'm not sure if it really happened or if it is a figment of my over active imagination enhancing the experience, but I believe we saw mountain goats with majestic curved horns. A magnificent sight indeed.

After the rain/snow storm, good weather was with us as we continued west through Cody, Wyoming, Buffalo Bill country, and into the Shoshone Valley.

We noticed as we drove along that car loads of travelling families would pass us several times a day. This came about since we would drive at a constant slower pace, and as they would make more frequent stops for meals and gas and the like, the cars would overtake and pass us several times. Every sign from these motorists was positive.

Our daily schedule called for early up – breakfast – break camp – getting underway – gas stop – sandwiches for lunch made and eaten en route – fairly early evening stop – set up camp – evening meal – early to bed.

Between Cody and Yellowstone, we shared a campground with another group of fellows travelling much like us. They were okay but we didn't really make an effort to be friendly, which we all felt was being prudent.

Yellowstone National Park, one of our premier stops, was next. We camped here for several days and made side trips, saw bears, and ate well; also did some hiking. A college boy from Medford, Brooks Conrad; an acquaintance of ours, was working at the concession at Old Faithful and we did get together with him for a visit one evening.

The wonders of Yellowstone, Old Faithful, the thermal pools, the wild life, the forests, the waterfalls, all nature were outstanding sights. Even though I had visited these areas with my parents several years earlier, everything again was delightful.

After our stop at Yellowstone, we proceeded on to Salt Lake City. Since the days were very hot at that time of the year, we decided to drive at night during the cooler hours. Here my chronology may be faulty but generally correct. As I remember during this night drive, one of the few mechanical problems occurred. A condenser in the ignition system failed and consequently the engine misfired, making progress impossible. Our first decision was to put up our cots in the desert and wait for sun up. It rained! Out in the arid desert it really rained, and also in the dark we had inadvertently place our cots near a dead rabbit. It was impossible to sleep. Bill decided to reduce the gap on the spark plugs and we then limped on to our nearest aid.

We did find help at an all-night filling station. After replacing the faulty part, we proceeded on to our destination. We arrived in the center of Salt Lake City very early in the morning. Fortunately, there was a public park just waiting for us to put up our tent and get some sleep. Soon after we had pitched our tent and crawled onto our cots, we were disturbed by someone shaking our tent. A policeman wanted to know what we were doing erecting our tent in a central city park. We had made a very honest mistake. In our hometown, overnight camping was allowed in the city park.

After explaining this to the officer it was accepted that we weren't just some wise-acre kids, and he suggested that we could find proper camping facilities up in Little Cottonwood Canyon.

This night of misadventure continued. After finally setting up camp in a designated camp site three of us turned in for much needed rest. Bill, however, decided it was time for a bath. A short distance up the side of a hill was a little stream which Bill decided was deep enough for his bath. The stream actually happened to be an aqueduct for Salt Lake City municipal water supply. Fortunately, there was no serious consequence and we did finally get sufficient rest to prepare us for the next night drive west over the Salt Flats.

We were acquainted with stories of Sir Malcolm Campbell's Blue Bird racer and his attempts to set speed records on the Bonneville Salt Flats. This interest demanded a stop at the race course area on our way to Carson City.

I must report an incident on myself. During the tedious night drive, we were doing one of those straight long hills and I thought this was a good time to allow the car to coast and save gas. When the other fellows realized I was doing this, I was duly admonished for a very imprudent action.

The next few days are a sort of blur, again my chronology is faulty. Putting nickels into a slot machine in Harold's Club in Reno (rather adventurous), a hurriedly set up camp with no tent in Bear Tooth Mountains, waking to a very cold mountain breeze, a drive on to Lake Tahoe, a very early morning swim in chilly Lake Tahoe, are all a vague and jumbled memory.

San Francisco was a high point of our experience. Our first view of the Pacific Ocean. Reaching the psychological half-way point of our journey made an indelible impression. San Francisco the City of the great earthquake and fire, Treasure Island with the excitement of the World's Fair, and structures like the Oakland Bay and Golden Gate bridges were awesome sights. Two of my lasting personal experiences were "Number one; questions formed in my mind of the significance of the huge hanger-like structures which housed many of the fair exhibits on Treasure Island; could these big buildings have been constructed in anticipation of future military usage? The accuracy of this observation was realized by me when several years later as a new Naval Dental Officer I was stationed at the huge Naval installation on Treasure Island.

The second recollection which is quite poignant deals with the City of Chicago exhibit at the Treasure Island Fair. The elaborate demonstration portrayed Chicago as being a very dynamic and vivacious city, and included a book into which exhibit attendees were asked to write their comments. I read some of the entries, one of which told the whole story. It simply stated, "I've been there." I felt what a great comment and then noted that it was signed Wm. Armbrust, Jr. I knew the person who wrote this succinct statement.

We were late in leaving the fair and since we realized that it would be very difficult to locate a motel we drove into the hills above Berkeley and slept in the car. This was the only time on the entire trip that it was necessary to sleep in the car.

Following an uncomfortable night, we started out the next morning toward Modesto to visit one of Mrs. Armbrust's chums from Academy days. Bill's mother had alerted her friend that we would stop for a visit. The family treated us well, they had planned a neighborhood cookout and fed us very well. We probably stayed for several days.

Yosemite and Sequoia Parks were next on our itinerary. Yosemite National Park was another of the prime experiences of the trip. We hiked up to Vernal and Nevada waterfalls along beautiful trails. We took photos of Half

Dome and enjoyed evening campfires. We watched the "fire fall" and thrilled to Jeanette MacDonald singing "The Indian Love Call". We joined some young people from the Los Angeles area at a dance in the Visitors Center. Lionel Hampton played the Vibraharp as part of the entertainment and we shared ice cream treats with some of the young group. People found it difficult to believe that we were from a different part of the world – Wisconsin!

The next happening as we continued south, was the drive through the huge evergreen trees of the Sequoia Forest. It really was neat, we literally did drive through the base of one of the big trees.

After a delightful stay in Yosemite and our visit to the Sequoias we carried on to the Los Angeles area. This was an eye opening experience. We saw an oil well in the middle of the highway, we bought ice cream by the quart at a very reduced price, and we were astonished at all the people. We visited my mother's aunt who lived in Hollywood. She fed the hungry campers and arranged for a day's visit to a movie studio. Her husband took us on a sightseeing excursion around Hollywood and the surrounding area.

After all this activity, it was time for a rest. We camped at a public beach near San Clemente for several days.

The highlights of the rest area: we made a large sand sculpture which attracted the attention of passengers on a passing train; we purchased, prepared and ate a large meal of corn-on-the-cob; and we visited with a work group which was policing the beach area. This visit allowed us a chance to get acquainted with the signs of our times. The work crew was a group of mostly Midwesterners that had migrated to California, the land of sunshine and plenty, just after the great depression. They were unable to get work and were listed on welfare roles. Being able-bodied they were placed in a labor camp. One of the group was especially interesting to us. This man was dressed in a white shirt and dark trousers which were quite worn but clean, his shoes were black leather, polished but badly cracked. He was conspicuous not only because of his dress (the other men in the work gang wore work clothes) but he opted to look busy but actually did almost no work. He was a great talker and spun a sad story about his plight. I guess we all learned an important lesson from this experience.

Since during our stay on the beach we were so close to Mexico it was important that we make our journey international. We drove to Tijuana and had our one excess of the trip: a glass of beer at what was reputed to be the longest bar in the world.

When we drove from California into Mexico, we had a large bag of plums. On returning to California, we were informed the fruit would have to be confiscated (agriculture laws). Rather than forfeit the plums, we ate them all before crossing back into the U.S.A. This may not have been such a wise move.

The poverty and desperation of the people in Tijuana was another encounter for us all.

A vacation trip had also become a great learning experience for kids leading a relatively sheltered life.

Las Vegas was reached by another hot desert trip, but I hardly remember any discomfort. Here we took a guided tour of the recently completed Boulder Dam (now known as Hoover Dam).

A visit to a guild hall introduced us to the world of Technocracy. Basically the tenets of this society was creation of machines to do the work, freeing up laborers for more recreation time, which could be enjoyed since production would be so outstanding, industry would pay higher salaries for less work. Thus the employees would have more money to enjoy recreation. This explanation was reminiscent of Mr. Guy D'Razio, our high school civics teacher who delighted in saying, "All these crazy schemes like Marxism and the others are just about perfect on paper."

Another observation made while touring Las Vegas was the fact that the many Oriental tourists, supposedly Japanese, with expensive cameras were constantly taking pictures of each other with the new Las Vegas Civic Center Building in the background. Possibly if our West Coast was under attack would this extensive building complex be used as a military headquarters for the Pacific Coast area. This again was speculation of an overactive imagination.

The trip was now turning towards home. Visits to Zion Park and Bryce Canyon were the next events on the itinerary.

At Zion National Park, we climbed Angels Landing, listed as a four and one-half hour strenuous hike. Here our canteen was useful as a water supply to preclude dehydration and also serve to wet our headgear. We covered our heads with handkerchiefs to serve as kepis to ward off the sun and keep our heads cool.

Earlier, a water bag was mentioned as part of our original equipment. An explanation of its function should be presented at this point. A water bag is an envelope shaped container made of tightly woven burlap. It usually was hung over one of the car's head lamps. The capacity is several quarts and it allows for some limited seepage through its walls. The seepage cools the contents by evaporation. The water in the bag probably isn't the best for drinking, but could be used as a cooling wash and for a water supply for the car's radiator. All during our drives in hot weather, a water bag was an indispensable part of our equipment.

Generally, our food was good, simple, but wholesome to our way of thinking. At Bryce Canyon, we had one of our food related problems. The morning pancakes were a disaster due to improper ratio of powder to liquid. Fortunately, food problems were rare.

Several memorable things occurred during a short span of time at this point of our trip. The drive through the Kibab Forest, north of the Grand Canyon, was very reminiscent of Northern Wisconsin. The sight and smell of the forest was refreshing. The view from the Canyon was outstanding, especially at sunrise and sunset. The view of Ship rock, that stirring sentinel, on the great desert created great memories.

My reaction at seeing Cliff dwellings at Mesa Verde was probably as thrilling to me as the reaction experienced by the ranchers that first stumbled onto the scene many years ago. On subsequent visits, I still experience a thrill when seeing these early dwellings.

Research indicates that the inhabitants of Mesa Verde were exposed to excessive tooth wear because of the high grit component which was present in their food due to the fact that they used sandstone implements to grind their grain. Also, study shows that the tribe medicine men drilled holes in the skulls of the mentally ill in an attempt to allow bad spirits to escape. Some skulls show several holes. It appears that in some instances healing occurred by acceptance of the small pieces of shell or hammered silver used for skull repair.

Going home ----

Mr. Hackbarth must have been checking road conditions because Ruben received a letter warning us about detours in Kansas. The detours had extremely rough surfaces and consequently the cause for our only tire problem. The constant micro shock from the rough surface caused rim pinch which resulted in a flat tire.

The other things about Kansas were notable, huge roadside billboards advertised local funeral directors, and a city named Athol. How embarrassing it must be to say, "I come from Athol, Kansas!"

The last area of historic and natural interest that we visited was St. Joseph, Missouri, located on the Missouri River. We stopped here to visit Ruben's aunt and uncle. Not only did they feed us well, but also introduced us to the history of the Pony Express and the Oregon Trail.

One little experience that must be related took place in Iowa. Apparently, there had been a prison escape and traffic was halted by a roadblock. Police officers inspected each car before allowing them to proceed. When it was our turn, the officer leaned into the car and asked for my driver's license, since I was in the driving seat. Not thinking, I reached under my shirt to get the license out. It was in safe keeping with the remaining funds in the money belt. The officer misunderstanding this movement quickly drew his pistol to the ready. Realizing what I was doing he relaxed and after being satisfied that we were not the culprits he sent us on our way.

We arrived back in Medford tired, probably hungry but quite well informed about the western portion of our nation.

During a period of six weeks, we had driven approximately eight thousand miles with practically speaking no mechanical or road problems. Our itinerary took us to a number of National and State Parks as well as many other points of interest. It was really quite an experience for four young lads. Above all, we had a story to remember and tell.

Werner John Pflughoeft – Storyteller

Father was a great 'story teller'. Not a raconteur but an honest-to-goodness storyteller. Most of his stories related to his experiences as proprietor and half owner of a small town furniture store and funeral home, a usual business combination in rural mid-America. One group of stories he told centered around his friends and fellow business owners who enjoyed pranks on each other, all very harmless but clever. A prime example: A nice old gentleman operated a small grocery store on Main Street. He was over anxious to be a good proprietor and aimed to please his customers and consequently the ideal victim of practical jokers. Occasionally after a light night snow several of his neighbors would make a point of arriving at their place of business earlier than the grocer and make footprints in the new snow leading up to the front door of the grocery store. When the unsuspecting grocer arrived to open his business at the usual time it appeared evident that disappointed customers had attempted to enter but found the door locked.

This of course bothered the victim of the prank and during the day he lamented to his neighbor proprietors saying, "My, oh my, they came early this morning." Consequently the next morning he would open his business half an hour earlier than usual much to the delight of the pranksters. The victim would then comment to his neighbor proprietors, "I was here early this morning and no customers came."

This story is relatively simple but difficult to relate – Read Closely!

One of the local druggists was a straight laced sort of stodgy old store owner, again a likely victim of a practical prank. For his benefit when he was present several of the guys would make a point of saying to friends entering their stores, "Close the door" in a rather gruff voice. This was all done in anticipation of setting-up the druggist for the inevitable faux pas. The druggist was a little myopic and his usual position in his store was behind the counter which placed him at a disadvantage as far as lighting conditions at the entrance to his store. And so it happened that as the druggist was tending his counter a person who had the build and carriage similar to the local banker, a friend of the druggist, entered the store, the druggist hoping to be clever and considered one of the bunch, sang out, "Close the door." The prospective customer replied, "Yes, sir. And from the outside." This of course upset the druggist and he scolded his friends for their treatment of persons entering their places of business.

All the stories had a much more interesting and humorous ring when Father told them because he knew the people in the stories: Mr. Gruber the kindly grocer, Mr. Benn the store druggist, Vince Hirsch the banker, Roy Musselman the baker, Charlie Fleming the bank president, a long list of really good friends and companions.

Mr. Musselman was the proprietor of the local bakery and grocery store. He was really a great character. His only failing was a very touchy stomach, which reacted uncomfortably for Muzz (as all his buddies called him). The buddies would make comments frequently to aggravate Mr. Musselman's problem.

Musselman's bakery-grocery store had an area with several small tables and chairs a place where the group of merchants occasionally met for a refreshment-coffee and rolls. Prior to one of the meetings Mr. Musselman concocted a plan for revenge to repay his friends for the misery they caused him by some of the remarks they made which were designed to upset his stomach. On that morning after the men had gathered at the bakery for a little conversation Mr. Musselman complained that he smelled something foul. After several such complaints he suggested that the members check their shoes to see if someone perhaps had stepped in some dog do. Everyone complied by sliding back in their chairs and inspecting their shoes – everyone including Mr. Musselman. Surprisingly Muzz aid, "Well, look at that! It's on my shoe." After a few seconds he said, "It sure looks and smells like dog do." Swiping his finger on his shoe and placing his finger in his mouth, he stated, "and it tastes like it too!" This of course broke up the gathering and caused each guest to experience varying degrees of discomfort. Mr. Musselman was gleeful about his revenge. Not until much later was it common knowledge that Muzz had softened a ginger snap and placed it on his shoe.

Another story about Mr. Musselman and Father describes a friendly confrontation between the two of them. It must be remembered that most of the members of the group of business men were also hunting partners that would frequently go camping and hunting and fishing together. Before construction of the Ho Hum (another story) camping meant tent camping. After one of these outings Mr. Musselman couldn't find his tent and he felt it had been mixed up with Father's gear. He asked Father several times to check to see if he did indeed have the missing tent. Whether Father looked or just ignored the friendly joshing about keeping someone else's equipment we really don't know. We do know that Muzz kept insisting and Father kept ignoring. After several weeks of banter Mr. Musselman involved the local County Sheriff by asking him to search our garage for the tent in question. The Sheriff realized his involvement in a prank, called Father and told him about Muzz's request. This was taking place during the time of prohibition and our family had homemade near bear stored in the garage. On receiving the call from the Sheriff, Father immediately called Mr. Musselman and told him the Sheriff had conducted a search of the garage and confiscated the near beer. Several minutes late Mr. Musselman was seen driving his car in the direction of the Sheriff's office. The conclusion of this involved prank is left to imagination of the reader.

Another lesser but related and equally as clever, a story about the 'hunting gang' involves Medford's other druggist. The gang was all assembled at one of the members' summer cottage for a feed. After the meal was finished the druggist, who was an amateur photographer, suggested a picture of the group in front of the fireplace. The fire was stoked up to hot and people and camera equipment arranged. After placing everyone close to the hot fire and taking an extended period of time fiddling with the camera settings the men became impatient and hotter and started to complain about the length of time to accomplish the setup. The photographer drew out the confusion subjecting the posers to discomfort for as long as possible and then apologetically announced, "Golly, fellas, I forgot the film." Whether true or not, no one ever saw a picture of the hunting crew around a roaring fire.

Dr. Stan O'Malley and his wife were friends of our parents. Stan had worked with Father in the store and funeral home while he was a high school student and the friendship continued. They visited often and every time they visited this story was repeated. Bordering on the macabre it still must be considered humorous. Father was called to a farm home on the death of the family patriarch. In those days the deceased was embalmed in the home and the body was arranged in a proper casket and set up in the living room, several days before the scheduled funeral. This all being accomplished Father announced to the family that the remains could be viewed. He left the farm house and returned to Medford. The funeral was to be conducted at the farm house in two days. Father felt good that he had done a proper job embalming and arranging the body in the casket. When he returned to the farm house to conduct the funeral he received quite a shock. Horrors! The body was in the casket but certainly not as Father had arranged it. Wow! He couldn't for the life of him come up with an answer. Had the body moved, certainly he was dead and embalmed, what had happened? The funeral was completed to the family's satisfaction but the mystery still existed – most unsettling. Subsequently Father fretted and dwelt on seeking an answer to what had happened. Several weeks following the funeral a neighbor of the dead man's family came into the furniture store. He said, "Pflughoeft" (in those days calling a person by his family name was accepted as a form of respect.) "Pflughoeft," he said, "I must tell you a story." He then related this. The family of the dead farmer had called upon this man to come to the house and bring his camera. The family didn't have a photograph of the father, and maybe they had feelings of guilt. To remedy this they had removed the dead man from the casket, placed him in a chair to have a photograph made with the family arranged around the dead father. The picture was taken and the remains returned to the casket, obviously not quite in the same position as originally placed by Father. The mystery was solved, the dead farmer had not moved on his own volition and the worry was over.

Stories Told by our Father Fondly Referred to as Oupa
By Frederick A. Pflughoeft
December 2002

Printed in the United States
By Bookmasters